EQUAL CH,

Eliminating discrimination and ensuring equality in playgroups

PREFACE

Social inequalities are deeply rooted in British society, influencing every aspect of people's lives and attitudes. From an early age British children are damaged by, for example, the racist, sexist and classist behaviour, images, attitudes and language that they see and hear around them. Although the consequences for black and for white children, for girls and for boys or for children with disabilities are different, **all** children are at risk and we need to intervene.

Equal opportunities policy statements endorsed by the Pre-school Playgroups Association include policies on anti-racism, anti-sexism and attitudes to disability. *Equal Chances* is designed to help groups which are working to put those policies into practice.

No book could ever be the last word on such a subject, and a successor is already planned. The second volume will contain the real-life, practical experiences of groups implementing equal opportunities policies. If you try out the ideas in this book; if you reject them and try out other ideas; if you add to them in your own way or adapt them to suit your local needs, **please let us know.** Write to the Publications & Periodicals Editor at PPA National Centre (address on back cover) and tell us how it worked. *What did the children say? How did the adults react? What were the successes and failures? How did you adapt your methods in the light of experience?*

This book has been written by a group of PPA volunteers and staff, with the help of colleagues within and outside the Association. The next book should be written by playgroups themselves, as a record of their work to ensure equal opportunities for children and families everywhere. Please respond.

Cover photograph by Margaret Hanton
Drawings by Tony Benjamin

i

EQUAL CHANCES

Eliminating discrimination and ensuring equality in playgroups

CONTENTS

PLAYGROUPS

Because they aim to meet the needs of all the under-fives and their families in all the communities within which they operate, playgroups can take many different forms. These are some of them:

■ **Playgroup** - a group offering sessional care for children mainly aged three to five years of age cared for with or without parents, no session lasting more than four hours. A few call themselves 'nursery' although they are registered as playgroups.

■ **Parent and toddler playgroup** - a group of parents or carers with children under school age, most of the children below the age of three. These groups provide for both children and adults. Parents remain with the child(ren) throughout the session.

■ **Under fives playgroup** - a group offering sessional care for children mainly aged three to five years of age, cared for with or without their parents. Children under this age also attend with a responsible adult who remains throughout the session. No session lasts for more than four hours (ie a playgroup and a parent and toddler playgroup running a combined session).

■ **Opportunity playgroup** - a group that is set up primarily to provide for children with disabilities or learning difficulties alongside other children. The children often start at an earlier age than in a regular playgroup and staff usually have more specialised training in this field.

■ **Family centre** - a group that offers opportunities for families to attend sessions, as and when they wish, with children of any age. Family centres often provide specific advice and counselling sessions for parents.

■ **Full daycare playgroup** - a group that accepts children under the age of five, without their parents, for more than four hours in any day.

■ **Creche** - a group which provides occasional care for children whose parents are on the premises but not present in the group.

The list above is not exhaustive. There are many other variations and combinations of groups which cater primarily for pre-school children and their families, including groups in hospital wards/clinics and on playbuses.

Although this book was written with playgroups in mind, its recommendations apply equally to under-fives provision in day nurseries, nursery groups/classes, etc.

TERMS USED IN THIS BOOK

Black: We have used this term to describe all ethnic groups in the UK who suffer discrimination because of their skin colour.

White: We have used this term to describe all ethnic groups of European origin who are disproportionately represented in positions of power and influence in the UK.

) We have used these
) simplified terms as
) a convenient shorthand.
) It is not our intention
) to diminish or disregard
) the many differences
) between and within
) cultures.

Prejudice:

Preferences, attitudes, judgements and opinions formed without adequate knowledge or reason.

Discrimination:

Unfair or unequal treatment of individuals because of their identity - ie their gender, ethnic group, class, disability, etc. (Some forms of discrimination, in addition to being morally wrong, are also unlawful. See Appendix 3 on page 43 for the relevant legislation.)

Stereotype:

A generalisation - often derogatory and based on prejudice - about any group. It can be used to prejudge a whole group on the basis of one individual and it can also focus the preconceived views of a group on an individual.

Whenever the word **parent** is used in this book, it should be taken to mean **parent or carer,** as parents are not necessarily the only adults who care for and have responsibility for young children.

INTRODUCTION

Children have a right to grow up and learn in an environment free from prejudice and without discrimination. We know that without this freedom their development will be damaged:

- Children who grow up feeling that they are inferior - or that other people see them as inferior - because of their gender, skin colour, disability or family background will fail to achieve their full potential.

- Children who are allowed to assume superiority because of their colour, their gender, their religion, their able-bodiedness, their class or for any other reason will have a false and damaging view of humanity.

- **All** children are damaged by attitudes and assumptions which fail to address in a positive way the differences which exist between us.

The playgroup can be the starting point in a child's journey towards self-esteem and an understanding of others.

Research* shows that children as young as two years do notice differences in physical appearance, such as skin colour. Soon afterwards children are attributing values to these differences; a person with a dark skin is often seen as less important than someone with a light coloured skin, or as someone to be feared. These values are learnt; children are not born with them. They are learnt from the people close to them and absorbed from the evidence of their eyes and ears as they observe our unequal society.

Joining parent and toddler playgroup, playgroup or any other pre-school provision is likely to be among a child's first experiences of society outside her/his family . This places a special responsibility on all playgroups to make sure that the environment and curriculum provided are free from the prejudice and discrimination which remain widespread and to provide positive images of all the adults and children living in our society.

This publication offers playgroups many examples of equal opportunities in practice. It is important to remember that equal opportunities is not just a matter of buying new resources; it is above all about attitudes and feelings, beginning with our own. All the specialist equipment in the world will not make a child with a disability feel valued and respected if she is offered pity but not expected to achieve realistic goals. What use is a dual language book to a child if she knows that her language is looked on as "nonsense" and her clothes as "weird"? What benefit does a young boy get from the dressing-up clothes if he is called a "cissy" and laughed at if he wants to try on a dress or a sari? How can a lesbian mother participate in the playgroup's activities if she feels that her sexuality is mistakenly equated with sexual abuse?

*Children and race: ten years on - David Milner (Ward Lock 1983)

Because of this, groups embarking on equal opportunities practice for the first time will need to consider before they start what they are hoping to achieve, what changes they plan to make and the reasons behind these changes. It is not a commitment which can be entered into casually; its implementation will affect every aspect of the group's life. The principles behind an equal opportunities policy have to be spelled out and the criteria governing future decision-making carefully thought through and agreed by the group. Ideally, these considerations should be combined in a written Equal Opportunities Policy which can be circulated to all the families in the group and given to any new families before they start to attend.

Without this framework for action, attempts at change may not prove successful and could even be counter-productive. If for example black dolls, or pictures of women in jobs traditionally done by men, or dressing-up clothes from a range of cultures are introduced without preparation or explanation, the effect may be simply to puzzle the children. The new materials may be mocked or dismissed, so that they - and the people associated with them - are even further marginalised.

An agreed action plan is necessary also to provide the support which all the adults will need when it becomes necessary to tackle any breaches of the group's policy. Many women, in particular, have been conditioned to believe that it is wrong (ill-mannered or un-ladylike) to upset the social apple-cart by challenging other people's behaviour and attitudes. They may be told they are "making a mountain out of a molehill", "getting hysterical" or "only making things worse". Believing in what you are trying to do and joining together with others working towards the same aims is the best defence against these accusations.

Equal opportunities are for everyone:

■ Children growing up in largely all-white areas still need the chance to understand that they are part of a multi-racial society.

■ Children who appear very happy to accept stereotypical male/female roles in their play may benefit from encouragement to try other approaches.

■ Children who have never encountered anyone with a disability can nevertheless be helped to think about what it might be like to have a body which does not always work perfectly.

In essence equal opportunities is about seeing and accepting the individual child/ family and making sure that everything possible is done to give that child/family the chance to develop their full potential in an atmosphere of mutual respect. We need to enjoy what we share in common, and to take pleasure in exploring the differences which make our society so richly diverse and exciting. Taking pride in ourselves and in our culture is not the same as believing it is superior to other people's. By enabling our children to understand this, we will be helping them to work for a more just and peaceful world.

CHAPTER 1

FEELING GOOD

In order to value others, we must first value ourselves. Children and adults need to feel good about themselves and secure in their sense of identity. Our sense of ourselves is reinforced when the people around us:

- acknowledge our existence and lifestyle
- listen to us seriously
- take account of what we say, either arguing with our suggestions or acting on them
- remember our names
- show affection for us
- like being with us.

We are all different.

We are different sizes, come from different backgrounds, have different religions - or none at all - are different ages and come from different ethnic groups and different classes.

Some of the differences are easy to talk about; others may make us feel uncomfortable and so we avoid them. Our discomfort may arise from feeling that our own class, sex, colour or ability is best. We need to overcome this in order to talk openly with the children. Children need opportunities to discuss and acknowledge the similarities and differences between themselves and their friends and neighbours. Discussions which take place in a positive way result in children having good feelings about themselves, feeling neither inferior nor superior to others.

Acknowledging difference is not the same as being prejudiced. Prejudice is learned, often at a very early age. Open, positive discussion can help children - and adults - to unlearn it.

Children are well aware of what is important to the adults around them. They pick up messages from all of us, from what we say and also from what we do not say. It is not necessary for adults to say that they dislike or disapprove of something; they have only to persist in never mentioning it. For this reason we have to make the opportunity to speak about the colour of people's skins, the different ways our hair grows, the fact that people wear different clothes, eat different foods, celebrate in different ways, speak different languages, have different abilities and come from different family backgrounds. We need to be able to give correct answers to children's questions about these differences and to help them understand that, although human beings have many important things in common, the differences between them are a source of great richness and variety.

1

I know the names for at least some of the feelings I experience and I know other people can feel that way too.

People remember my name and call me by it, spelling and pronouncing it properly.

My opinions are sought and respected and I feel free sometimes to say NO.

I feel at ease about my own body, its size and colour and shape. I know that it is like other people's bodies in many ways, and in some ways different. I know that some parts of it work better than others, and that this is so for other people too.

I know that I like some things better than others and that some of my friends agree with me and others feel differently.

I FEEL GOOD

My family are acknowledged, welcomed and asked after.

People say 'Hello' to me and smile.

Things which are important to me, such as my birthday, religion and culture, are acknowledged and, if appropriate, celebrated in the group.

Adults listen to me when I talk to them and take what I say seriously, giving me plenty of time to think through what I am trying to tell them.

I know what things I am good at and I am encouraged to feel proud of them and to use my skills to help other people.

Practical Activities

These are some suggestions for activities which can support the development of children's self-esteem. They are by no means exhaustive and you will be able to think of many other things to do. As with any other playgroup activities, the adults will offer these ideas at appropriate times, to extend children's play and thinking, or to add a new dimension to it.

Feelings

Small children have strong feelings and need opportunities to talk about them, to give them names and to recognise that other people have them too. Children might be invited to draw a happy or sad face on a paper plate. The adult can then write underneath. ADAH FEELS HAPPY WHEN...her dad takes her to the park/ she gets to the top of the climbing frame/her friends come to visit. SAM IS SAD WHEN...his baby sister is crying/he can't go out to play/his mum is cross with him.

Make sure there is enough time really to listen to what each child is telling you. Don't be afraid to share your own feelings as well, if there is an opportunity.

Bodies

Young children's bodies are very important to them. Their natural interest and curiosity can be used to help them understand:

- that their bodies belong to them; nobody has a right to intrude on them without permission.

- that bodies, and the various parts of them, are similar in many ways and different in others.

- that boys and girls are different, but both boys **and** girls can be strong **and** gentle, agile **and** slow, and that all of these qualities are valued.

- that parts of some people's bodies work better than, or differently from, others.

These are some of the activities which can focus children's interest in bodies:

- Let the children use a mirror to look at themselves and their friends and to compare their hair, skin and eyes.(Encourage them to be exact: skins are not just "brown" or "white" or "black".)

- Make sure the group offers paint and paper in a full range of skin colours so that the children can paint accurate pictures of themselves or their friends.

- Explore what it would be like not to be able to see or hear or walk without aid.

■ Make a collage from pictures of faces, as many different ones as possible. Stick a small mirror in the centre and see if the children can find in the collage someone who looks like them.

■ Write positive statements on life-size drawings of the children: *Helmut has new shoes; Katie likes her pet rabbit; Judith can build tall towers with the bricks.* (Most under-fives will not be able to read much except their own names, but there will be plenty of adults to read them out, which will help confirm children's understanding of the connection between the written and the spoken word as well as boosting their self esteem).

■ Children can be helped to make books by doing drawings or paintings of themselves, their families, home, friends, toys and pets. Underneath each picture can be the words the child wants to say, dictated by the child and written down by an adult. The pictures can then be tied or stapled together and the cover could have a photograph of the child and/or her/his name, very clearly and colourfully written.

Being special

In some playgroups, when the children are gathered together, the playleader chooses someone different every day to admire, saying their name and what it is that is special about the child that day: **Antonio is looking very nice today; I do like your green socks.** If you try this, you might have to keep a note to make sure nobody is missed out. (Try it with the adult helpers as well and see the big grins!). Avoid complimenting girls only on their personal appearance; boys only on strength and skill.

Draw T-shirts and let the children each decorate their own. Put them on a wall for all to admire. Add a line that says, "I AM GOOD AT...."

Things I like

Being free to express opinions and preferences is one important aspect of a sense of personal identity. If you build up a bar chart for the wall showing, for example, the children's favourite foods, you will be helping their mathematical understanding as well as reinforcing their right to be different from one another. Alternatively individual children, or the whole group, can be invited to contribute pictures or examples of things they like (or dislike) for a collage or scrapbook on a particular theme such as toys or pets. If you embark on a project like this, be sure to allow plenty of time for discussion in very small groups so that everyone gets a chance, and is encouraged, to express an opinion.

Names

Names are an important part of people's identity. Both children and adults should be addressed by the names thy want to be known by. The Registration Form will include the full names and titles of parents/carers and children, but it is a good idea also to make clear the name the child is known by, including any abbreviations. (If the child whose registered name is Catherine is usually called Katie, neither the sound of the name nor the initial letter will be familiar to her.) If possible, write children's names down - correctly spelled and in their original alphabet too where this is not English - and put them on display.

One group decorates a paper plate for each child who comes. It remains on display, with the child's name in the middle, for as long as the child is attending the group. It is a friendly acknowledgement of the special importance of each individual child as well as a useful spelling aid for adults.

Families

A collection of photographs makes a good starting point for talking about families. These can form the basis for a project which might involve:

■ Making a scrapbook/collage of pictures of the families in the playgroup

■ Talking about the generations in families, from baby brothers and sisters to grandparents/great grandparents

■ Looking at animal families and the different ways in which they live

■ Reading together stories which include the variety of families

■ Discussing the many forms which families can take

■ Recognising that the households children come from may include one or two parents; adults who are married, unmarried or remarried; a gay couple bringing up children; brothers/sisters, step-sisters/brothers or no siblings at all; two or more families living together; extended families; foster parents; friends living together.

Food

Let the children cut out pictures of favourite food from magazines and stick the cut-outs on paper plates. Provide a wide enough range of food pictures to illustrate the many different kinds of food and the different ways of cooking and presenting it. Try to include illustrations showing that people in different cultures may eat in different ways, with different implements, and help the children to understand that no one way is better than any other.

Buy a different fruit every week and let everyone have a chance to feel, smell, taste some. If possible, find a story, picture or puzzle with that fruit represented.

Bring in a selection of vegetables to smell, feel, cut up and cook. *What happens to the vegetables when they are cooked?* (Keep some raw pieces back for comparison.)

Invite children to describe, compare and discuss the foods they have at home, both every day and for special occasions.

Do they, or other people at home, have a special diet to keep them well?

How many different sorts of bread can you buy, or make in the group?

Some of these activities are more difficult in largely white rural areas. A special trip to town might be necessary to make sure that the children do not miss out on a range of new experiences and the understanding that can grow from them.

Celebrations

The pattern of the year, changing seasons, major family events and, in some families, religious observances form an important part of children's lives. These events need to be acknowledged in the group. Talk about the things people might celebrate and feel happy about. At home, this might be a baby's first word. In the playgroup, it might be a new piece of equipment.

Why not plan a celebration in your group, inviting the children to discuss

What they would like to celebrate

What people might want to wear

What kind of food there could be?

The parents in the group might have information about festivals they have taken part in or about special-occasion food they can provide. Beware of making assumptions, however, about families' religious/cultural backgrounds. People who belong, or seem to belong, to the same cultural or religious group might still

6

choose to behave quite differently in many ways. Black or Asian families might be Hindu, Buddhist, Moslem, Christian or Sikh or have no specific religion. White European families are not necessarily Christian and some Christians (eg Jehovah's Witnesses) do not celebrate any festivals. It is important to avoid stereotyping and to talk to the families in the group to find out what they **really** like and want.

Ways of celebrating might include:

■ Decorating the room

■ Decorating the people (by dressing-up, face-painting, hand and foot-painting, wearing masks)

■ Having a procession

■ Using the images of light which are common to many festivals.

If you are celebrating a festival with which you are unfamiliar, make sure you research it thoroughly by talking to people who understand its significance. Think carefully about the way you will introduce the festival to the children so that they understand the story behind it. (Make sure parents are informed in advance if you plan to celebrate any religious festival so that other arrangements can be made for those who may not wish to take part.)

Even if your playgroup families all come from the same cultural group, the children need a chance to begin to understand the wider world in which they will be growing up. Giving them the opportunity to understand and enjoy other people's festivals can help counteract some of the negative impressions they may already have picked up elsewhere, as well as being a lot of fun. In addition, activities like this extend children's vocabulary and broaden their general knowledge and understanding.

CHAPTER 2

FAMILIES IN PLAYGROUP - A SENSE OF BELONGING

If all families are to feel "at home" in our playgroups, each group must deal with three aspects of being at home:

1.   Feelings

People who feel "at home" feel at ease, among equals, confident about their own role and value, accepted for what they are. Every family should feel like this in playgroup.

2.   Homes reflected in play provision

Every playgroup contains many representations of homes and families: in songs and stories; in pictures on jigsaws, books and posters; in dressing-up clothes; in the presentation of food; in the home play area itself. All children and families should find in the playgroup something which resembles their own homes.

3.   The home outside the playgroup

People's homes are the base from which they operate and the root of their confidence and self esteem. Even home situations which are physically or emotionally undesirable/damaging are still an important aspect of the lives of the people concerned.

If they are to be 'at home' in the playgroup, families must feel that their own homes and lifestyles are accepted by the group. All families should feel that their approach to such matters as clothing, child-rearing practices, food and religious festivals is acknowledged by the playgroup.

These are some of the ways in which we can help families to feel "at home":

■   People's attitudes to the group can be set long before they visit it or talk to the people in it. Make sure that outside publicity materials - posters, leaflets and pictures -reflect all the communities in the area served by the playgroup and include a statement about the group's equal opportunities policy. In some areas, it might be necessary to produce materials in more than one language.

■   There is no such thing as a 'normal' family. Avoid presenting children and their carers with assumptions about families.

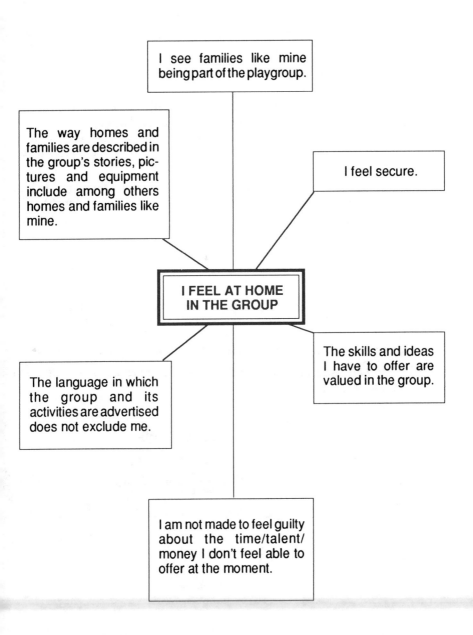

I see families like mine being part of the playgroup.

The way homes and families are described in the group's stories, pictures and equipment include among others homes and families like mine.

I feel secure.

I FEEL AT HOME IN THE GROUP

The skills and ideas I have to offer are valued in the group.

The language in which the group and its activities are advertised does not exclude me.

I am not made to feel guilty about the time/talent/money I don't feel able to offer at the moment.

You will need to look at:

- Stories* and pictures in the book corner. (Do they always present families as having a mother, a father, a detached house, two children - one male, one female - and a dog?)

- Pictures* on jigsaws/posters.

- Messages home. Are they always addressed to "Mr & Mrs...."? Not all children have two parents; not all parents are married to one another; not all married people use the same name; not all families have the Western European naming system of individual forename plus shared surname. Find out what people want to be called and how they wish to be addressed.

- Gifts made by the children. It may not be appropriate for all children to make cards for "Mother's" or "Father's" Day and not all families will welcome cards celebrating the festivals of religions they do not subscribe to. A simple "Love to....from...." is usually enough.

■ Home is a place where you expect to come and go freely and where you have a right to be. If the playgroup is to be genuinely 'homely' for all the families, you will have to make it easy for them to be there.

- Parents may need to bring younger children with them if they are to be fully involved. Is there some space for buggies/prams? Is there something safe and appropriate for little ones to do? (Don't forget to check the position of 'extra' children with the local authority which registers you.)

- Adults with disabilities may need special help - or wheelchair access - in order to be present.

- Not all families use European style furniture. If some of the families in your playgroup prefer to sit on the floor, do you provide rugs/cushions/ a clean floor?

*See page 15 and 16 for more details about these activities

■ People at home together share out the work. Each benefits from having the support of other family members and from the satisfaction of doing their share. People gain a lot in playgroup too from taking their share of the work and the responsibility. The opportunity to do so needs to be open to all.

- Adults who cannot be present during the playgroup day/session, perhaps because they are at work, should not be criticised or excluded because of this. They can become involved in other ways. They could for example be asked to choose library books, make/maintain equipment, help with a special event or offer ideas/suggestions. A written equal opportunities policy will make clear people's right to be involved and the framework within which things are done. People choosing books or pictures, for example, need to know in advance the principles on which the group operates and the criteria used to select equipment.

- One way of accepting and exercising responsibility in a playgroup is by joining the management committee, so the times and places of Committee meetings must be convenient and suitable for everyone. (The room above the pub might rule out parents with a disability, Moslems and Free Church members. Holding meeting in people's homes might be cheap, but it can exclude people who feel they cannot offer such hospitality and may make some others feel uncomfortable.)

- Travel to meetings may be a problem. Sharing transport can help.

- For families new to the playgroup, the first opportunity to become involved in the management of the group is often at the Annual General Meeting.
Make sure all families are able to take part by

❏ giving them plenty of notice of the date, time and place, in the language they most comfortably read.

❏ arranging the time so as not to exclude working parents.

❏ helping single parents if necessary by assistance with baby-sitting arrangements or by welcoming children, either in the meeting itself or in a small creche.

❏ arranging a venue with wheelchair access if necessary.

❏ making sure everyone, including newcomers, understands what is being reported/discussed. This means avoiding jargon and allowing plenty of time for questions/explanations.

■ People feel at home when they can share in the fun as well as the work.

- Outings should take heed of the tastes and abilities of all the families in the group

- If there are parties/refreshments, the foods should represent all the cultural traditions and diets in the group.

- Take the opportunity to learn about and perhaps celebrate all the religious/cultural festivals observed by the families in your group.

■ The people actively involved in the running of the playgroup should represent as many as possible of the various communities in the area served by the group. To make this possible, you may need to take steps to ensure:
- that training is available to everybody, subsidised whenever possible
- that everybody knows about the training and is told about it in their own language
- that your procedures for appointing staff are fair and open, designed not to discriminate - even unintentionally - against any section of the community. If members of a particular racial group are under-represented in the work in question it is lawful for an employer (in this case the playgroup) to encourage applications from persons of that group or to make training available specifically for them.

CHAPTER 3

CREATING AN ENVIRONMENT

An equal opportunities playgroup will be one which is rich in opportunities for each child to explore her/his identity and to build her/his self-esteem, free from false expectations and from attitudes which would limit development.

The group will also be one which looks outwards to its local community and to the wider world, so that children can begin to develop an understanding that there is no one 'right' culture but many changing cultures to which everyone, regardless of ability, gender, race or colour has a contribution to make. This diversity is a source of richness to be greatly enjoyed.

The first step must be to ensure that the group meets the needs of all the communities in the area it seeks to serve and that the children and families who attend come from all the local communities.

If all children are to have an equal chance to attend the group, all families must have an equal chance to find out about it and use it. This has implications for the places and languages in which the group advertises and for the way the waiting list is organised. A 'first come, first served' system, which might seem so fair at first glance, can exclude a lot of people. See Appendix 1 for details of the PPA Information Sheet on Admissions. The Registration Form included in the PPA leaflet, *Our playgroup* has questions which will help you to compare the ethnicity of playgroup registrations with the patterns in the locality and also to check the families who initially register against those who finally attend. If local authority figures show, for example, a large number of Afro-Caribbean families in the area, but none register for the playgroup, or if none of the Asian children who are registered ever take up the places which become available, you need to investigate.

Positive action may have to be taken to ensure that *everyone* with small children *knows* that the playgroup will welcome their particular family.

■ Liaison with local Health Visitors may reveal the existence of mothers/fathers who, perhaps because of depression or other disability, would have difficulty in finding out about or making contact with the playgroup.

■ The Health Visitor or Social Services Department may be aware of people on the fringe of the local community, such as Traveller families, who may not know about the playgroup or who may be unsure about how to approach the group and the kind of welcome they will receive there.

■ PPA Guidelines recommend that children with disabilities and learning diffi-culties should be considered as a priority for admission to the group if the parents wish them to attend. The parents of a child with a disability may need specific reassurance - perhaps via a health visitor - that their child will be welcome and perhaps that an extra helper will be available if necessary.

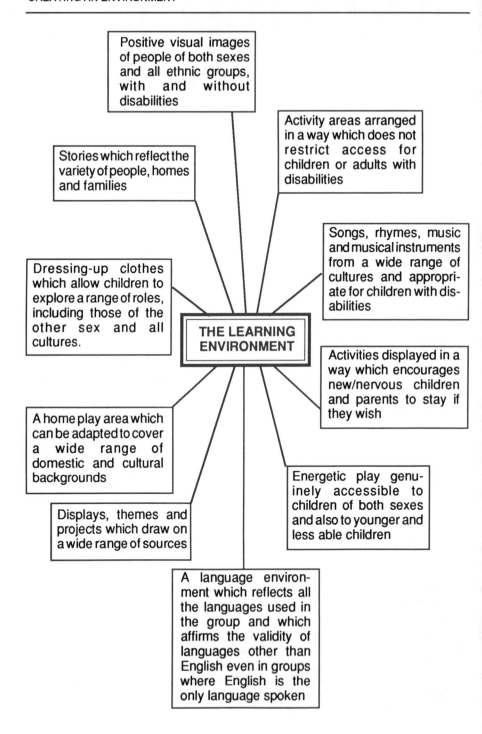

Positive visual images of people of both sexes and all ethnic groups, with and without disabilities

Activity areas arranged in a way which does not restrict access for children or adults with disabilities

Stories which reflect the variety of people, homes and families

Songs, rhymes, music and musical instruments from a wide range of cultures and appropriate for children with disabilities

Dressing-up clothes which allow children to explore a range of roles, including those of the other sex and all cultures.

THE LEARNING ENVIRONMENT

Activities displayed in a way which encourages new/nervous children and parents to stay if they wish

A home play area which can be adapted to cover a wide range of domestic and cultural backgrounds

Energetic play genuinely accessible to children of both sexes and also to younger and less able children

Displays, themes and projects which draw on a wide range of sources

A language environment which reflects all the languages used in the group and which affirms the validity of languages other than English even in groups where English is the only language spoken

People will want to join a group only if it values them. The group needs to be seen as a place which (a) has adopted an equal opportunities policy and (b) *practices* it.

Once children have been admitted into the group, it is important to ensure that the environment created there will allow all children to flourish and that the things they learn as they play will nourish their self-esteem and their awareness of others as well as supporting their intellectual and physical development.

An equal opportunities approach is a continuing process, not a one-off event, and has implications for the way we look at and present all play activities, all the time:

Books and storytelling

Stories and pictures presented to children should depict a world in which both boys and girls, old and young people, from all ethnic and cultural groups, whether or not they have disabilities, have positive qualities and are capable of dominating the action. All groups should have at least some books:

■ in which black children take the lead rather than being present as background figures or not present at all;

■ in which girls initiate action and help other people rather than waiting to be rescued;

■ in which people with disabilities attract interest and respect as well as sympathy;

■ in which families other than the Western European nuclear family are seen as viable - and as having a good time together.

These positive images are necessary to develop the understanding of all children, whatever their own colour, sex or background. Books which present a narrow, stereotyped or patronising view of any social group should be discarded. (Although playgroups hate to throw anything away it is important to destroy such materials, not to pass them on to others.)

Although most pre-school children cannot read, they are learning about language from the books which adults choose to make available to them. Books with bilingual texts can help all children to understand that there is more than one written language in the world and that they can all tell stories equally well. If there are any children in the group whose first language is not English, of course, it is essential that they see their home language acknowledged in the playgroup. Parents and playgroup leaders can be reassured that this will not hinder the children's learning of English. On the contrary, confidence in the first language is an essential foundation for success in the second.

For children leaning English as a second language, and also for children of varying age and ability, frequent small story-telling groups are more pleasurable and more effective than daily full-group storytimes. Small groups can take account of the children's different language levels, which is especially important for children with learning difficulties. Small groups also provide a good opportunity for stories/rhymes in languages other than English.

If possible introduce the children to some of the specialist languages such as signing and Braille. Many groups are able to draw on the expertise of parents or other members of the local community to illustrate the use of these. (Young children, whose fingers are softer and more sensitive than those of adults, are often surprisingly quick at recognising Braille letters). Signing can be great fun. Try introducing the children to the sign for *playgroup.*

Reproduced by kind permission: Positive Images

Visual images

Books are not the only source of the many visual images we as a society present to young children. Their picture of the world is built up also from pictures on jigsaws, packaging and posters, in catalogues, magazines and other media. It can be difficult to ensure when using these resources that we do not create a false picture of a world in which: all senior jobs are held by men; all families comprise mother, father and two children; black people are successful only as sports people and entertainers; all little girls wear pretty frocks; everybody is full of health; Janet helps Mum in the kitchen while John helps Dad clean the car!

Groups deliberately trying to counteract these images may find it helpful to write for catalogues from manufacturers of equipment for the disabled and for posters from organisations such as the Commonwealth Institute. The Working Group Against Racism in Children's Resources (address in Appendix 2) has a list of organisations producing posters which show positive images of all children. Quite a lot of packaging of household goods and foods now include instructions in a range of languages and these can be used in the home play or junk modelling areas of the playgroup as appropriate to extend children's understanding. Beware of campaigning posters which show black families only as victims of poverty and famine and in need of help. Many black people, in Britain and elsewhere, are successful, independent and well-educated with a lot to contribute to the societies in which they live. Both black and white children need to be aware of this.

16

Spoken language

The overall noise level should allow all children to be **heard.** This is especially important for very young children, for those in distress or with hearing problems and for children who may be learning one or more languages in addition to English.

For children whose home language is not English, it can make a lot of difference if the staff enlist the parents' help if necessary in acquiring at least one or two phrases in the child's home language, including the words children use for relativesand family members and daily words such as *hungry, toilet* etc. This validates the child's own language and strengthens the links between playgroup and home. It also gives children a refreshing view of the adults by showing them trying to learn a new skill and, probably, not doing it very well at first. (People with a traditional English education are often at a disadvantage here. Many Asian families speak several different Asian languages as well as English, whereas few English children and adults speak more than one language.) There should if possible be an adult present who speaks the home language of each child, but this does not mean that other people should not try too. It is not unlawful to seek a particular language speaker in order to meet the special needs of a particular racial group.

It can be illuminating for children to listen to someone talking to them in a language they do not understand and then to discuss how this makes them feel.

Simple dolls and puppets representing a range of racial and cultural backgrounds and carefully selected to avoid stereotyping give children the opportunity to engage in story-telling or role play in their home languages.

Home play

If children are to enjoy rich imaginative play in the home play area, the area must be capable of looking something like home to each child. For example, it should be possible for the table and chairs to be put aside in favour of floor cushions for children whose own homes are organised that way. Other examples include Asian, African or Chinese cooking pots as well as European ones; African as well as European-style combs beside the mirror; and chopsticks in addition to European cutlery.

In this area of activity, especially, children encountering unfamiliar equipment from other cultures will need support in understanding that items which appear strange to them are not 'odd' or exotic, but are used in an everyday fashion by thousands of people in Britain and elsewhere.

The contents of the home play area can be given a multi-cultural flavour by the use of pictures, wall-hangings, packaging showing other scripts/languages and perhaps envelopes with foreign stamps on. Coins from other countries can be added provided that young/immature children are well supervised and not at risk from swallowing them.

Groups which make 'food" for use in the home play area should make sure it includes a range of food: chapatis as well as sliced bread; samosas as well as chips; spring rolls as well as sausages. This applies to all groups, whatever their own ethnic composition. **All** children need to know about the multi-racial society in which they are growing up.

Dolls should be available for use by boys as well as girls and should include male as well as female, black as well as white ones. When buying black dolls, check that the features and hair are appropriate for the skin colour. Some black dolls give very confusing messages by having European features and hair, but black skin - or even black faces and pink bodies.

Dressing up

Dressing-up activities are important because they offer children the opportunity to explore through role play the way they see people and what it might be like to be someone other than themselves. For this reason, the dressing-up clothes must offer a wide range of options, with clothing connected with both sexes, a range of occupations and as many different cultures as possible. Some parents may have to be reassured that there is nothing wrong in children dressing up as a person of a different sex or culture and that this exploration of other roles can help extend children's understanding of themselves and of each other.

There is a place in playgroup for 'special' clothes from any culture to be brought in, discussed and admired. The clothes in the dressing-up corner however should represent also the everyday clothes worn in daily life throughout the world.

With the clothing, as with the cooking equipment, children presented with an item which is totally unfamiliar need to be helped to see how it is used so that there is no risk of their dismissing it as 'silly'. Books and posters can help here, as well as input from parents and others in the local community.

In playgroups which include families from several ethnic groups, the children's parents will be a useful source of advice and may be able to help ensure that dressing-up clothes, for example, are authentic. (Bear in mind that an adult sari will swamp a child. A child's sari is about three metres long but you should be able to make four by cutting down an adult one). Playgroups which cannot draw on local resources will have to use specialist supplies and to seek advice on the presentation and use of multi-cultural equipment. (See Appendix 2 for useful addresses).

Energetic play

Just as some discreet stage-management may be necessary to ensure that boys as well as girls really are free to use dolls, so adults will have to be alert to prevent the possibility of the physical play equipment being dominated by a group of well coordinated, active boys. The boys have a right there of course - and a right, too, to even more challenging physical activity under proper supervision if their stage of development requires it - but the climbing frame, wheeled toys etc should be available also to other groups: younger children; new children; girls; children with disabilities.

Occasionally this can be achieved simply by finding an attractive new occupation for the usual 'tenants' of the climbing frame and waiting for the other groups to move in. However, it might not be as simple as that. Even very young children can arrive in the group having already got the message that there are things they do not do. They may have already been told too often that "Girls don't do that" or that "You might get hurt" or "You won't be able to manage that". Such children may have to be supported in discovering for themselves what they can do and enjoy, rather than what they cannot.

If the children's own parents have given them these negative messages, perhaps

19

in order to protect a child with disabilities or to bring up a girl to behave 'properly', careful discussion with the parents will be necessary to protect the child from being at the centre of a conflict of attitudes. This is one of the many occasions when a written Equal Opportunities Policy can be a very useful document to refer to. It will put into words the thinking behind the group's policies and, if it is distributed to all families, it will give the parents an idea in advance of the way the group is run.

Stereotyped assumptions about boys in general and Afro/Caribbean boys in particular can result in their being left to pursue energetic activities without being challenged in other ways. **All** children need a balanced range of activities:

- solitary play *and* the company of adults
- competition *and* cooperation
- the development of gross *and* fine motor skills
- the pleasure of involvement in active games *and* encouragement to listen and concentrate.

Messy play

This is yet another area of activity from which some children may be excluded by the attitudes and expectations they bring with them. Quite a number of children grow up with the feeling that anything which threatens the cleanness of their hands, clothing or bodies is *'naughty'* or *'nasty'*. Such feelings can be very deeply rooted and must never be dismissed or overridden by the adults in the group. At the same time, these children are sometimes the very ones who could most benefit from the release of messy play.

Really efficient protective clothing can set at rest the minds of some children and their parents. Other families may choose to bring the children to and from playgroup in smart clothes but allow them to change into old clothing for their time in the group. For Afro-Caribbean children with tightly curled, braided and/or oiled hair, getting sand out of the hair can be difficult and painful. If they are to be free to join in sand play, some form of head covering must be readily available for anyone to use. (Hats or headscarves, at the sand tray or in the dressing-up corner, must be cleaned regularly.)

Sometimes the emotional difficulties are more difficult to overcome than the practical ones and some children need a very gentle introduction to messy play. Techniques which may help them to overcome initial feelings of fear and revulsion at the prospect of being dirty are:

- clear starch, uncoloured, for finger painting
- pastel colours at the painting easel
- well-kneaded, non-sticky, pastel coloured playdough
- a smallish piece of clay, soft enough to handle but not wet and sticky, away from the messy clay table.

Music

Of all playgroup activities this is perhaps the one which demonstrates most clearly the advantages of living in an area in which the songs, rhythms, rhymes and instruments of a wide range of cultures are readily available. Groups for whom this is so should make full use of their good fortune. Parents and others from the local community will be able to show and demonstrate the use of a wide range of musical instruments and children will be delighted to learn one or two songs in a language other than their own.

Groups which cannot draw on such rich local resources should still be able to introduce a range of other kinds of music, if only by means of recorded music and pictures of instruments.

It can be especially satisfying to a child with a physical disability to have a group activity in which s/he can participate on completely equal terms. For children with learning difficulties, the rhythm and repetition of playgroup songs and rhymes can help them to join in the fun.

There is strong commercial pressure to make us think that all young people can respond only to pop music. Playgroups are a place where this pressure to limit children's understanding and enjoyment can be resisted. Children can enjoy and should be offered, in small doses, all kinds of music; both folk and classical music from many countries, as well as the sounds of brass bands and music from dance and opera.

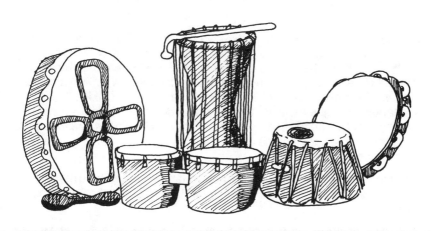

If there are instruments for the children to play, ensure that girls as well as boys have a turn with the noisy ones.

21

Themes, projects and displays

The existence and importance of both sexes, of all peoples, of people with and without disabilities should be affirmed through all activities. A display on vegetables should include okra and mooli as well as parsnips and cabbage; scrapbooks on clothing should show shalwar kameez, khurtas and wrappers as well as trousers and skirts; references to sports and hobbies should cover both polo and pigeon fancying, as well as contests for people with disabilities.

Cooking

Here too some playgroups will be able to draw from their families an exciting range of possibilities to offer the children. Other groups can still broaden their scope by the use of recipe books. There are some suggestions in the Appendix.

Conversation

If we respect children, we must allow them space to reflect, to consider viewpoints/information they have not encountered before, to come to their own conclusions and to discuss these openly with trusted adults. Try holding regular sessions at which children and adults can raise and ask questions about issues of concern. This can give children a forum for their own feelings and can indicate to the staff which subjects need to be addressed as well as opening up possibilities for other activities or project work.

CHANGES

By implementing all the suggestions in this chapter, the group will have gone a long way towards creating a learning environment which can enrich the lives of all the children, but that is not the end. However much care and thought have gone into arranging the activities there will always come a time when the needs of the children - or of one particular child - will demand a change or adjustment to the way you do things. Only a constant awareness of the needs and rights of each new child and family coming into the group can ensure that the group continues to offer equal opportunities for everyone.

The suggestions in this chapter are only a start and you will find many other ways of creating a learning environment which can enrich the lives of all the children.

Whatever methods you adopt, they will need constant change and adjustment if the group is to meet the needs of each successive generation of children and families and to go on ensuring equal opportunities for everyone.

22

CHAPTER 4

WORKING TOGETHER - ADULTS SHARING SKILLS

Playgroups can be vitally important for parents as well as for under-fives. Many parents find in playgroup the support they need to help overcome feelings of isolation and begin to feel a part of their local community.

Parents' rights

"Certain parental rights should be considered as part of a definition of quality of care because this enables parents to influence the nature of their children's care environments. To this end the following opportunities for parents should be considered:

❑　to acquire information about the care environment

❑　to express their views on the care environment

❑　to alter the care environment of their child

❑　to contribute to their child's care environment

❑　to choose between alternative childcare environments.

This approach enables parents to have some choice over divisions of their time between parenting and other activities. Access to services, choice between services, transport to services and hours during which care is available are all relevant for parents wishing to make informed choices."

Extract from the Department of Health's Guidance and Regulations on the Children Act - Volume 2: Family Support, Day Care and Educational Provision for Young Children.

The aim must be to create a group in which:

■　everyone feels they have a part to play

■　their views and opinions are considered and accepted or rejected courteously and thoughtfully

■　their values, religion, language and culture are respected and welcomed.

This is not easy. It will be easier if the rights of parents are acknowledged and structures are put in place to ensure these rights are met.

But the systems will not work properly without the right attitudes behind them. Whatever their theoretical rights in the group, parents are always well aware of whether their input is really welcomed. Playleaders, owners and committees need to recognise that knowledge is power and to enjoy sharing both. People who like feeling that what they say goes, or that they know what's best and should be trusted to get on with it "properly", may find it difficult to run a group where everyone has an equal chance to contribute. People in charge of groups should enjoy acquiring knowledge and skills and be able to discuss and share these with others, coming to agreement through consensus about what they mean for the whole group.

Acquiring information - communication

Ownership of the group by its members depends on adequate communication systems.

Parents and playleaders alike must be encouraged to share as much information as possible with each other. (There should be clear rules about what types of information shall remain confidential and to whom. Each group may evolve its own policy on this in order to ensure that the wellbeing of the child and the parents is paramount at all times.)

Communication, to be effective, must be a two-way process. It must not only be a means of making information available to everyone involved in the group so that they can accept and understand it; it also should encourage questions and contributions that will further thinking.

All policies, committee decisions that affect parents and children, rules or regulations the group has made should be written into a clear and easily understood parent booklet and given to each parent when a child is registered at the group.

The booklet should include details of the management of the group, the names of the playleaders and committee members, information about parent involvement, suggestions about clothing for children and a host of other things which you will find itemised in PPA Guidelines publications*.

Some parents will want to take the booklet away and discuss it at home, coming back with questions. Others may have difficulty in reading, or in reading English, and you will need to be alert to this possibility because parents will not necessarily mention it.

The booklet should, if necessary, be written in a number of different languages. If this is not possible and it is not available in the language one or more parents most readily read, an interpreter should be found and time spent in explaining the booklet more fully.

Opportunities should always be offered to talk through any aspect that needs clarification or causes concern. The booklet should be regularly updated, with parents being asked to contribute, and new issues should be given to all parents at the group each time it is produced.

Good practice for sessional playgroups. Good practice for parent & toddler playgroups.
Good practice for full daycare playgroups.

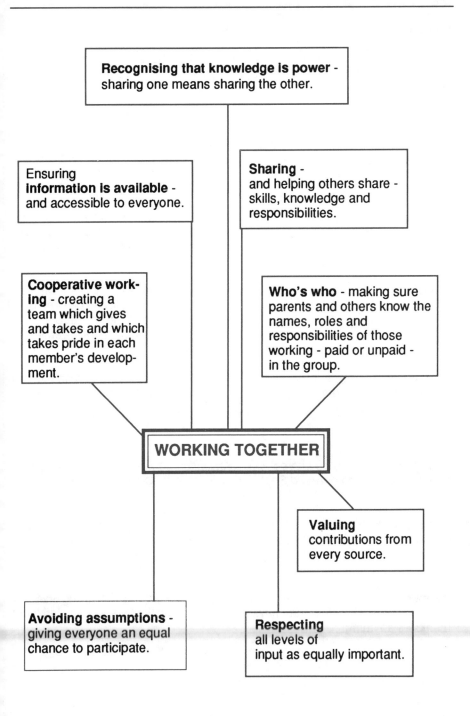

Recognising that knowledge is power - sharing one means sharing the other.

Ensuring **information is available** - and accessible to everyone.

Sharing - and helping others share - skills, knowledge and responsibilities.

Cooperative working - creating a team which gives and takes and which takes pride in each member's development.

Who's who - making sure parents and others know the names, roles and responsibilities of those working - paid or unpaid - in the group.

WORKING TOGETHER

Valuing contributions from every source.

Avoiding assumptions - giving everyone an equal chance to participate.

Respecting all levels of input as equally important.

Getting it across

On a day to day basis, making sure everyone has the same information is hard, but very important. Some systems of passing on information are clearer than others!

Unclear system	*Clear system*
Information passed on verbally by several people with no way of knowing who has said what to whom.	Information passed on verbally by one or two people with lists of names to check off.
Speaking to the person who collects a child without giving written information to pass on, where necessary, to parents.	Telling the person who collects a child and also giving written information to pass on the parents.
Posting information on the notice board but then placing the board where only the parents who come into the playroom can see it.	Making sure the notice board is in a place where it can be seen by all parents and other people - and alerting people to the need to look at it.
Detailing someone to pass on information by phone. (Not everyone has a phone).	Using both letters and phone, with a checklist to ensure all are contacted.

In preparing notices, as in producing information booklets, you need to ensure that people who do not read English do not miss out on information.

The *key worker* system recommended in PPA Guidelines avoids many of these problems by ensuring that responsibility for communication with a small number of families lies with a single key worker.

It is easier if you work out a system for ensuring that information-giving works for all, and then use it, rather than having to rethink each time you want to tell group members anything.

Remember not to assume anything

assumes that new members know where, at what time and for how long the committee meets

assumes that all families know when half term is - including those whose children do not yet go to school or do not attend local schools.

Try to put yourself in a new member's shoes and ask yourself, "Is what I've written/said intelligible to someone who doesn't know the ropes? Does it give them everything they need to know in order to act upon it?"

Valuing contributions

If you are successfully sharing information and encouraging feedback and the expression of views, you next need to ensure that people are thanked for making their views known and that they know all ideas and comments are welcome and considered. It is important that changes made as a result of what has been said or suggested should be acknowledged. The thinking that everyone has a part to play in creating the best possible environment, that two heads are better than one, that we all have different needs that are legitimate, will then be constantly reinforced.

Staff too need to be sure that their contributions are welcome. Regular staff meetings offer people opportunities to raise issues at an appropriate time.

It is worthwhile exploring whether the person who made the suggestion would like to contribute to making it work. (We all make suggestions from time to time about jobs we would really like to do ourselves!). There are always jobs to be done in the group - in addition to those mentioned on page (11), they include being Treasurer, compiling and updating an inventory of equipment, organising fundraising, keeping the waiting list, reclaiming the milk money and representing the group on the Branch Committee as well as being on the parent rota. Make sure people get a chance to change though - some people may be happy left with the milk money for ever; others will be dying to get the dressing-up clothes sorted instead. Opportunities should be found for the development of new skills and interests and to cater for a growth in confidence and abilities.

Delegating work is an art. If you are to be successful at it, you must be happy for things to be done differently from the way you would have done them yourself. You will need to accept new ways of doing things and perhaps some feeling of loss of control. You will have to judge when to remind and when to trust. You will occasionally have to pick up the pieces. The compensation and satisfaction come from watching others take up responsibility and grow in confidence and self esteem. Try to involve everyone while recognising that not everyone can contribute in the same way. Teamwork counts, and all contributions are valuable. Some people work better in twos; others may find helping impossible for periods of time - perhaps when there is a new baby or a domestic crisis. Language difficulties or disabilities may mean a parent will need extra support to take on a task. The important thing is that the door is left open and offers are welcomed.

Avoiding assumptions

How often have you thought - "We can't ask X to do that because...."?

FACT	ASSUMPTION
- she's got four children	(therefore hasn't got time)
- he hasn't got a car	(therefore can't get there)
- she goes out to work	(therefore is too busy)
- she's a granny, after all	(therefore is too old, not capable)
- he's a single parent	(therefore has child care difficulties)

Making assumptions like this is not fair and may not be accurate. Such assumptions are based on prejudice and stereotypes. It is important to give everyone an equal chance to be involved with the group. The best thing is to check whether people wish to do something but be willing to accept if they do not.

Some assumptions are mistaken because they are based on inadequate information. It is sometimes assumed, for example, that children and adults with AIDS or who are HIV positive pose a risk to others in the group.

In fact, children and adults with AIDS or who are HIV positive pose NO RISK TO OTHERS provided that recommended hygiene rules are observed. Both children and adults who are HIV positive benefit from a reduction in isolation so long as they are well enough to attend the group.

28

Knowing who's who

A booklet about the playgroup (page 25) will help new parents to begin to find their way in a system which might be quite new to them.

There is no substitute however for personal introductions. New parents need to meet the committee/owner as well as the staff. The more people they know, and the more they understand about the various roles and responsibilities in the group, the easier it will be for them to approach someone if they have a problem or want to find something out. Some groups find it helpful to put up photographs of staff and committee with their names and jobs.

Giving people the chance to know one another is one more means of making them feel it is **their** group, one in which they have a right to contribute in their own way, as part of the team.

Through working together in this way many parents develop confidence and skills they never believed they had, which remain with them long after they and their children have moved on from playgroup.

CHAPTER 5

TAKING ACTION

Even in playgroups where equal opportunities practice is followed there will be times when hurtful or abusive remarks are made or discriminatory behaviour happens. Every playgroup needs to work out ways of dealing with these incidents. We have a responsibility to act, otherwise we are adding to the hurt or offence. Our silence will appear to condone the behaviour and people will assume that such behaviour is allowed, even encouraged.

It is not uncommon to be frozen by fear in these situations. We can be tempted to pretend we didn't hear or see and to walk away. This fear often stems from thinking that by acting we will make matters worse, and that we will not be able to deal with what happens. There is a lot we can do to overcome this fear.

A written Equal Opportunities Policy creates a framework within which to respond and can also help by putting into words the values you need to protect. It should be clear to all members of the playgroup that it is not acceptable to make fun of any aspect of a person's identity, such as their skin colour, their name, their disability, their gender, their religion, language, etc. Nor should anyone be excluded from taking part in the playgroup's activities for these reasons. Anyone who breaks the rule, adult or child, should be told that we don't allow behaviour or talk like that in playgroup and helped to see how they have given offence. This might be the first time their prejudice has been challenged; supporting them with explanations rather than blaming them personally is more likely to help them change their ideas and behaviour.

At the same time it must be clear to people, especially to the victim of such behaviour, that we are not excusing it, that we take it very seriously and don't expect it to happen again. Whenever such an incident occurs, support for the victim comes first. We will need to show that we care about their feelings by saying so. "I know it hurts when people call you names. He was wrong to say that and I will tell him not to do it again" - with a cuddle if appropriate.

Children should be encouraged to ask questions and should not be made to feel guilty for asking them on subjects which some adults find embarrassing. "Why is Yasmin's skin brown?" is not an offensive remark. It is a request for information and should be answered simply and honestly. "Yasmin's skin is brown because her Mummy and Daddy both have brown skin; your skin is pink because your Mummy and Daddy have pink skin." If we avoid giving straight answers to such questions, children very quickly pick up that there must be something bad about skin colour. (This applies also to other areas such as parts of the body, where babies come from, disabilities etc). If we don't know the answer to a question we should say so and say that we will find out or help the child to find out, but we should not use this as an excuse to avoid "awkward" questions.

HEAR
Don't let it pass
or walk away

LONG TERM
Plan work/projects to help
change behaviour and
improve understanding

RESPOND
Say at once that this
behaviour is not allowed
in playgroup

**DISCRIMINATION AND OFFENSIVE
REMARKS ARE DEALT WITH WITHIN A
FRAMEWORK CREATED BY THE
GROUP'S POLICY AND ALL MEMBERS'
KNOWLEDGE OF IT**

ACTION
Explain what was offensive.
Try to get understanding
and bring parties together

INFORM
Point out untrue
statements and give
correct information

SUPPORT
Let victims know you care about their
feelings and support them in standing up
for themselves

All staff in the playgroup will be expected to carry out the group's policies, on equal opportunities as on any other matter. If a member of staff fails to challenge discriminatory behaviour, the playleader and/or committee will need to find out why. More support and discussion may be necessary to help that staff member to gain confidence to assert the group's policies in future.

The diagram on page 31 is an action plan to help with responding to unacceptable behaviour. It's important that all the adults in the group feel able to do this. Practising together how you would handle different situations is good training.

Here are some examples reported by playgroups. You probably already do this kind of "What if...?" exercise in connection with accidents and emergencies, and know how it helps to build confidence in your ability to cope.

WHAT IF....
Mary says, "My daddy says I can't play with Celeste because she's black..."?

HEAR
This must be tackled straight away. Saying, "That's not a nice thing to say" is not good enough.

RESPOND
Ask Mary how she thinks Celeste feels and say, "I would feel sad if someone said that to me."

INFORM
Say, "We have a rule in playgroup that we all play together; we like having people in our playgroup who have different skin colours. I will explain our rule to your Daddy."

SUPPORT
If Celeste heard, comfort and support her immediately. Ask Celeste how she feels, helping her to put her feelings into words.

ACTION
Follow up with Mary's father. Explain what happened and what you said. Remind him about the playgroup's policy and ask for his cooperation. (If the playgroup's Equal Opportunities Policy, handed to all new parents, has at the end an acceptance section which Mary's parents signed when she joined, the group is in a stronger position.)

LONG TERM
Plan projects around skin colour, paints, self portraits, stories, pictures etc. Make sure posters and other visual resources present positive images of all children.

****

WHAT IF....
A parent helper says to a child after an accident, "Big boys don't cry..."?

HEAR
This may be a common saying but it needs challenging, not ignoring

RESPOND
"We try not to say that in playgroup because we want all the children to talk to us about how they are feeling. It's part of their learning."

INFORM
We all cry if we get hurt.

SUPPORT
Tell me how you got hurt. Let's go and find the first aid box for a plaster.

ACTION
Ask the helper if she can help the child feel better by encouraging him to choose something to do.

LONG TERM
Talk with parents about helping children to discuss their feelings, boys as well as girls.
Talk to children about what makes them happy or sad or want to cry.

****

WHAT IF....
One of your parent helpers has a disability. (Her arm is missing below the elbow). You hear one child say to another that she doesn't want Kim's mummy to help her put her coat on in case she touches her with her "funny arm"...?

HEAR
Don't be embarrassed to talk about disability.

RESPOND
Say you know Kim's Mummy's arm looks different but there is no need to be frightened, or make fun of her.

INFORM
If you know why the arm is like this, tell the child. If Kim's Mummy wants to, she could explain.

SUPPORT
Mention how pleased the playgroup is to have Kim's Mummy helping and talk about all the things that she is able to do despite her disability.

ACTION
Suggest Kim's Mummy demonstrates how she puts Kim's coat on.

LONG TERM
Explain to Kim's Mummy that you like to answer children's questions and not avoid talking about disability. Make sure that when she helps at playgroup she is involved in the children's activities.

Ensure that at least some playgroup books and posters show people with disabilities coping well with life.

****

WHAT IF...
One of your parents, hearing that there is to be an HIV positive child in the group, says "If you accept that child I will take my Joseph away."?

HEAR
This a direct challenge to playgroup policy and can't be fudged, though the parent's attitude can be understood in the context of fear and misinformation.
RESPOND
Explain that it is playgroup policy to be open to all families in the community. Say you would be sorry to see Joseph leave.
INFORM
State quite clearly that there is no risk to adults or children if recommended hygiene practice is carried out, and that you already follow this practice.
SUPPORT
Say that you understand her fears for her own child. Try to get her to see that your existing hygiene practice eliminates the risk from the child with HIV and from many other infections such as Hepatitis B.
LONG TERM
Arrange for a speaker from the Local Health Authority/Social Services to come and talk to a parents' meeting about AIDS/HIV.
Raise awareness of hygiene precautions by talking to the children about the way diseases are spread and the ways we avoid catching them,

****

Making changes in playgroup is never easy and taking action can make us feel very vulnerable as we are bound to make mistakes. Listen to people's comments, take time to think about them and to get over any hurt or anger and then try to talk it through with the person. Use constructive suggestions and, where possible, ask for the person's help. It is good to say when we think we were mistaken and what we have learnt from the mistake.

It helps a great deal to get support if people know what we are trying to do, and why. This is where a written Equal Opportunities Policy for the playgroup can be very useful, especially if everyone has been involved in drawing it up. The children too should be involved. They can be surprisingly clear about what is fair and unfair.

National PPA's policy statements on anti-racism, anti-sexism, disability and equal opportunities in employment are useful to refer to, as are the policies of your Local Authority and other organisations, but the playgroup's own policy can clearly set out its own aims and a plan of action to reach them. This policy can then be given and explained to every new group member. It should be regularly reviewed - possibly at each AGM - to incorporate new aims and note progress.

An equal opportunities policy can also be useful in dealing with other organisations. A Local Authority might expect to see a policy before giving a grant or allowing the use of their premises. Some Local Authorities may require an equal opportunities policy when registering groups under the Children Act. If playgroup premises are shared it may be necessary to approach other users and/or the landlord about improving the access to the building for the disabled, or about removing posters and other materials which are inappropriate or offensive. In all such situations, having a clear written policy will help to make the playgroup's case in a firm but calm way.

Aiming high is important but so is setting realistic tasks, starting with what people feel most able to tackle, sharing the responsibility and building on success. In this respect equal opportunities is no different from other aspects of playgroup work where involvement, training, learning and support are all part of good practice.

Appendix 1

BOOKS AND OTHER RESOURCES

a) For adults
Adults need materials which will make them alert to discrimination and which will support them in opposing it. The following might be helpful:

The anti-bias curriculum - Louise Derman-Sparks and the ABC Task Force (VOLCUF, 1989)
Tools for empowering young children

Let's play together - Mildred Masheder (Green Print, 1989)
Cooperative games for everybody

Educating the whole child - book and video (Building Blocks 1989)
A holistic approach based on equality and cooperation

Building for the future - book and video (Wiltshire PPA, 1990)
The broad spectrum of equal opportunities, filmed in playgroups.

Playing them false - Bob Dixon (Trentham Books, 1989)
Assumptions behind children's toys, games and puzzles

Keeping the peace - Susanne Wickert (New Society Publications, 1989)
Conflict resolutions with pre-schoolers

Festivals pack and **Activities pack** - (NES Arnold, 1988)
An activity-based approach to multicultural play

Open sez me - Shirley West, 67 Church Street, Brighton BN1 1RL (1990)
Practical ideas on a seasonal basis, covering over seventy festivals

From cradle to school - (Commission for Racial Equality, 1989)
Race equality and childcare

All children are special - (PPA Publications, 1988)
Children with and without disabilities in playgroups

Guidelines for the evaluation and selection of toys and other resources for children - (Working Group Against Racism in Children's Resources, 1990)
Choosing books and play equipment

The eye of the storm - video (Concord Film Council, 201 Felixstowe Road, Ipswich, Suffolk IP3 9BJ., 1973)
The development of racism in young children

Education for equality ed. Mike Cole - (Routledge, 1989)
Some guidelines for good practice

The SHAP calendar - published annually by Commission for Racial Equality
The dates and significance of festivals celebrated by all cultures and religions

All our children - (BBC Education, 1990)
Raising awareness of equal opportunities issues in childcare

Training for equality - (EYTARN 1991)
A pack for use by all trainers

PPA Guidelines - (PPA Publications,1989)
Good practice for sessional playgroups
Good practice for full daycare playgroups
Good practice for parent & toddler playgroups

Statement of principles - PPA Information Sheet No 2
Adopted by members at the AGM in 1989

Equal opportunities policy statements - PPA Information Sheet No 5
Policies on anti-racism, anti-sexism, disability and equal opportunities in employment

Helping the visually impaired child - PPA Information Sheet No 7
Support in playgroup for the partially sighted child

HIV and AIDS in pre-school groups - PPA Information Sheet No 8
Information, prevention and support for those affected

Helping the hearing impaired child - PPA Information Sheet No 9
Support in the playgroup for the child who is deaf or hard of hearing

Children with special needs in PPA playgroups - PPA Information Sheet No 11
The implications of the 1981 and 1988 Education Acts

Opportunity playgroups - PPA Information Sheet No 12
Children with and without disabilities playing and learning together

Welcome to our playgroup - PPA Information Sheets 16 - 22
Leaflet available in Bengali, Cantonese, English, Gujerati, Turkish, Urdu and Vietnamese

The Children Act 1 - PPA Information Sheet No 26
The implications for groups

Lone parents - PPA Information Sheet No 28
Single parent families in the playgroup

Admissions - PPA Information Sheet No 29
Ensuring that playgroups are genuinely open to all

Cooking around the world - Ealing PPA
Playgroup recipes from many countries

Pour the cocoa Janet - SCDC (Longmans)
Sexism in children's books

b) For children
A booklist for children can never be fully comprehensive, but every playgroup needs books which meet the following needs. The texts listed are good examples, but you may well have others which meet those needs in your group. Browse regularly in libraries and good bookshops so that you keep up to date with what is available.

BOOKS WHICH BUILD POSITIVE IMAGES

Franny and the music girl - Emily Hearn (Magi)
A very active heroine - in a wheelchair

Ben's brand new glasses - Carolyn Dinan (Faber)
A small boy comes to terms with a disability

Something else - Wendy Lohse (Hodder & Stoughton)
A hero without legs.

Come sit by me - Margaret Merrifield (Women's Press)
Set in playgroup, about a child with AIDS

BOOKS WHICH CHALLENGE STEREOTYPES

Drac and the gremlin - Allan Baillie (Picture Puffin)
The imaginary games of a fearless (female) warrior

Maurice's mum - Roger Smith (Picture Puffin)
A very funny defence of being 'different'

Are we nearly there? - Louis Baum (Magnet)
A little boy's outing with a loving dad who is no longer living with the child's mother

My grandma has black hair - Mary Hoffman (Methuen)
A grandmother who is not a sweet old lady

Prince Cinders - Babette Cole (Collins)
A variation on the roles traditional in fairy tales

BOOKS SHOWING CHILDREN AND FAMILIES IN A WORLD CONTEXT

A balloon for Grandad - Nigel Gray (Orchard Books)
Sam imagines how the balloon he has lost might travel far away to his Grandad
Abdullah.

Dear daddy - Philippe Dupasquier (Puffin)
The life of the father away at sea contrasted with the child's life at home awaiting
his return

BOOKS WHICH DEVELOP CHILDREN'S AUTONOMY AND SELF-ESTEEM

Feeling happy feeling safe - Michelle Elliot (Hodder & Stoughton)
Children from a range of ethnic backgrounds handling challenging situations with
success

If you meet a stranger - Camilla Jessel (Walker Books)
Olu keeps herself and a younger child safe by heeding the advice of her playgroup
leader

BOOKS WHICH INTRODUCE OTHER LANGUAGES

Imran's clinic, Gail's birthday and **Liam's day out** - Katie Teague (Magi)
Stories about children from various cultures, each available in dual language
versions: English with Bengali, Chinese, Greek, Gujerati, Hindi, Punjabi, Turkish,
Urdu and Vietnamese

Where's Spot? - Eric Hill (National Deaf Children's Society, 24 Wakefield Road,
Rothwell Haigh, Leeds LS26 0SF)
With parallel signed English translation of the text

Rosie's walk - Pat Hutchins (Random Century)
and
How do I put it on? - Shigeo Watanabe (Random Century)
Each of these popular classics is now available in a number of dual-language
versions

BOOKS IN WHICH CHILDREN FROM A RANGE OF CULTURAL BACKGROUNDS PLAY A LEADING ROLE

Rebekah and the slide - Christine Parker (Dinosaur)
A little girl of mixed race in a situation with which all children will identify

Evan's corner - Elizabeth Starr Hill (Viking)
An Afro-Caribbean child and his relationship with his younger brother

I don't care! - Errol Lloyd (Red Fox)
Children act out a traditional Jamaican rhyme

In a minute - Tony Bradman and Eileen Brown (Methuen)
Heroine Jo has a white father and a black mother. The book tells of a family outing with Sita from next door

BOOKS WHICH PRESENT A MULTI-RACIAL SOCIETY

What colour? - Fiona Pragoff (Gollancz)
Toddlers from a range of ethnic groups playing with everyday objects. Each page covers a different colour, including black

Nursery rhyme board books - photographed by Anthea Sieveking (Frances Lincoln)
Four books of traditional rhymes illustrated by photographs of beautiful babies of many different ethnic groups

Going to playschool - Sarah Garland (Bodley Head)
A playgroup, full of people of all colours, sizes and ages, having a good time together

One day at playgroup - Donna Bryant (Hodder & Stoughton)
Also about playgroup. This time Joseph's black mother is the helper

Alfie gives a hand - Shirley Hughes (Picture Lions)
Alfie overcomes his shyness at a party in order to protect Min

The singing sack - Compiled Helen East (A & C Black)
Songs and stories from many countries and cultures. Tape also available

Well chosen books can make an enormous difference to the children's developing understanding. However, with books, as with the other resources mentioned earlier, it takes the support of alert and sensitive adults to ensure that the materials achieve their full potential.

Appendix 2

USEFUL ADDRESSES

Commission for Racial Equality (CRE) - Elliot House,
10 - 12 Allington Street,
London SW1E 5EH

Equal Opportunities Commission - Overseas House,
Quay Street,
Manchester M3 3HN

The Working Group Against Racism - 460 Wandsworth Road,
in Children's Resources   London SW8 3LX

Voluntary Organisations Liaison - 77 Holloway Road,
Council for Under Fives (VOLCUF) - London N7 8JZ

Food Commission - 88 Old Street,
London EC1V 9AR

Centre for Studies on Integration - 415 Edgware Road,
in Education (CSIE)   London NW2 6NB

Health Education Authority - Hamilton House,
Mabledon Place
London WC1H 9TY

Multi-Cultural Education - Contact your local
Resources Centres   education department

Early Years Trainers Anti-Racist Network - 1 The Lyndens,
51 Granville Road,
London N12 0JH

Building Blocks - 40 Tabard Street,
London SE1 4JU

PPA Equal Opportunities - PPA National Centre,
Employment Group   61 - 63 Kings Cross Road,
London WC1X 9LL

PPA Equal Opportunities Development Group	-	PPA National Centre, 61 - 63 Kings Cross Road, London WC1X 9LL
Letterbox Library non-sexist and multicultural books via a book club	-	8 Bradbury Street, London N16 8JN
Childsplay a multicultural and non-sexist toyshop	-	112 Tooting High Street, London SW17 0RR
Magi Publications a publishing house concentrating on anti-discriminatory books for young children	-	55 Crowland Avenue, Hayes, Middx UB3 4JP
Commonwealth Resources Centre multi-cultural materials available on loan	-	Commonwealth Institute, Kensington High Street, London W8 6NQ
Rifton a catalogue of equipment for people with disabilities	-	Robertsbridge, East Sussex TN32 5DR
Access to Information on Multi-cultural Education Resources (AIMER)	-	Faculty of Education & Community Studies, University of Reading, Bulmershe Court, Earley, Reading LRG6 1HY
Council for Racial Equality/ Community Relations Council	-	Most areas have one Address from local authority or library
Mantra Publishing anti-discriminatory books and tapes	-	5 Alexandra Grove, London N12 8NU

Appendix 3

RELEVANT LEGISLATION

Disabled Persons (Employment) Act 1944 & 1958

Equal Pay Act 1970

Sex Discrimination Act 1975

Race Relations Act 1976

Education Act 1981

Disabled Persons Act 1986

Children Act 1989 + Guidance and Regulations

NHS & Community Care Act 1990

All available from HMSO bookshops

OTHER PPA PUBLICATIONS

What children learn in playgroup - a PPA guide to the curriculum

PPA Guidelines   Good practice for sessional playgroups
                          Good practice for parent & toddler playgroups
                          Good practice for full daycare playgroups

Play Activities   Glueing
                          Make believe play
                          Sand and water
                          Clay and dough

Learn Through Play   Maths through play
                          Language through play
                          Science through play

Starting a playgroup

The playgroup session - a guide for adults

Accident prevention and first aid

Playgroup register

Playgroup account book

Playgroup accident & incident book

Teenagers in playgroups

Leaflets   Settling at playgroup
                          Helping at playgroup
                          Our playgroup (with registration form)
                          Come to playgroup (for when a place becomes available)
                          PPA training.

*For a complete list of PPA publications and promotional goods,
send a SAE to:
PPA National Centre, 61-63 Kings Cross Road,
London WC1X 9LL.*